eat.shop twin cities 2nd edition

an encapsulated view of the most interesting, inspired and authentic
locally owned eating and shopping establishments in minneapolis and st. paul, minnesota

researched, photographed and written by anna h. blessing
cabazon books : 2010

table of contents

eat

shop

anna's notes on twin cities

I am thrilled to introduce you to the second edition of *eat.shop twin cities*. When I began the research for this edition it was still 2009, and the country was reeling. Let's just say it was a terrible, horrible, no good, very bad year. But you would have never known times were tough in Minneapolis and St. Paul. While the nation's knees were weakening under the pressure of it all, the stalwart, industrious folk of Minnesota seemed stronger than ever, friendly as always, and creating new, exciting places.

As I set out to explore new, noteworthy spots and rediscover old favorites, it became clear that things were a-hoppin' in these twin towns. *Rustica Bakery* was gearing up for a big move to its own space, Joni Wheeler opened the sweetastic *Sugar Sugar*, *moto-i* opened as the first sake brewery restaurant in the United States and Juan of *La Chaya Bistro* took a run-down Burger King and turned in into one of the stand-out new spots to eat in the city. I don't want to go on and on, but the list of new additions to this city's culinary scene is exciting! Meanwhile, *Wonderment* opened a second outpost of its wonderful toy shop, and classics like *Ingebretsen's* and *J.W. Hulme* kept going strong, while newcomers like *blackblue* and *Ladyslipper Boutique* show that this city not only has deep roots, but fresh new ones too.

As we were going to press though, some heart-wrenching news came our way. The block in South Minneapolis where *Blackbird*, *Heidi's* and *Shoppe Local* (and its sister store *Patina*) were all located, burned to the ground. In honor of these beloved businesses, we have kept them in the book, because we support them in their effort to open again! Watch their websites for information.

Outside of the world of eating and shopping, here are a few of my favorite things in the Twin Cities:

> *Guthrie Theate*: It's great to walk around Jean Nouvel's structure and enjoy the views of the Missis-sippi, but try to catch a show if you can.

> *Walker Art Center*: Amazing space with an stellar contemporary art collection (and good places to shop and eat while you're there!)

> *The Lakes*: There are lots of them here, and with a multitude of activities to enjoy, whether it's biking, picnicking, walking, boating or just admiring.

> *Mill City Farmer's Market:* Indoor/outdoor market where you can browse, sightsee and get a sense of the best of the best from Minnesota farmers.

about eat.shop

• All of the businesses featured in this book are locally owned. In deciding which businesses to feature, that's our number one criteria. Then we look for businesses that strike us as utterly authentic and uniquely conceived, whether they be new or old, chic or funky. And if you were wondering, businesses don't pay to be featured—that's not our style!

• A note about our maps. They are stylized, meaning they don't show every street. If you'd like a more detailed map, we have an online map with the indicators of the businesses noted > map.eatshopguides.com/twin2. And a little note about exploring a city. The businesses we feature are mainly in neighborhoods within the urban core. Each of these 'hoods (and others that we don't cover) have dozens of great stores and restaurants other than the ones listed in this book.

• Make sure to double check the hours of the business before you go as they often change seasonally.

• The pictures and descriptions for each business are meant to give you the feel for a place. Don't be upset with the business if what you see or read is no longer available.

• Small local businesses have always had to work that much harder to keep their heads above water. During these rough economic times, some will close. Does this mean the book is no longer valid? Absolutely not! The more you use this book and visit these businesses, the better chance they have to stay open!

• The *eat.shop* clan consists of a small crew of creative types who travel extensively and have dedicated themselves to great eating and interesting shopping around the world. Each of these people writes, photographs and researches his or her own books, and though they sometimes do not live in the city of the book they author, they draw from a vast network of local sources to deepen the well of information used to create the guides.

• Please support the indie bookstores in the Twin Cities. To find these bookstores, use this great source www.indiebound.org/indie-store-finder.

• *eat.shop* supports the *3/50 project* (www.the350project.net) and in honor of it have begun our own challenge (please see the back inside cover of this book).

• There are three ranges of prices noted for restaurants, $ = cheap, $$ = medium, $$$ = expensive

previous edition businesses

If you own the previous edition of *eat.shop twin cities*, make sure to keep it. Think of each edition as part of an overall "volume" of books, as many of the businesses not featured in this new edition are still fantastic. The reason earlier edition businesses aren't in this book is because there are so many amazing businesses that deserve a chance to be featured!

eat

al's breakfast
anodyne
bev's wine bar
black sea
cafe twenty-eight
candyland
cave vin
chocolat celeste
corner table
galactic pizza
grand cafe
lucia's
matt's bar
moose & sadie's
pop!
punch
sebastian joe's
ice cream cafe
spoonriver
tank goodness
tanpopo noodle shop
ted cook's
19th hole bar-b-que
the barbary fig
town talk diner
rue thai
victor's 1959 cafe
w.a. frost and company

shop

birch clothing
bone adventure
coe & channell antiques
corazon
danish bohemia
design collective
evla pottery
garden of eden
gather
heavenly soles
indigo
joynoelle
karma
rick rack
robot love
saga living
status
stephanie's
the yarnery
three pagodas
uber baby
up six
via's vintage
walker art center shop

If a previous edition business does not appear on this list, it is either featured again in this edition, has closed or no longer meets our criteria or standards.

where to lay your weary head

there are many great places to stay in the twin cities, but here are a few of my picks:

graves 601
601 north first avenue (downtown minneapolis)
612.677.1100 / graves601hotel.com
standard double from $139
restaurants: bradstreet crafthouse, cosmos
notes: modern design by michael graves

chambers
901 hennepin avenue (downtown minneapolis)
612.767.6900 / chambersminneapolis.com
standard double from $200
restaurants: d'amico kitchen, eden
notes: luxe art hotel

w minneapolis – the foshay
821 marquette avenue (downtown minneapolis)
612.215.3700 / starwoodhotels.com/whotels
standard double from $200
restaurant: manny's
notes: art deco cool

aloft minneapolis
900 washington avenue south (downtown minneapolis)
612.455.8400 / starwoodhotels.com/alofthotels
standard double from $179
restaurant: re:fuel (sm)
notes: the w's more casual sibling

the hotel minneapolis
215 fourth street south (downtown minneapolis)
612.340.2000 / thehotelminneapolis.com
standard double from $179
restaurant: restaurant max
notes: comfortable and stylish downtown spot

notes

112 eatery

one of the best places to eat in town

112 north third street. between first and second
612.343.7696 www.112eatery.com
mon - thu 5p - midnight fri - sat 5p - 1a sun 5p - 10p

opened in 2005. owner / chef: isaac becker
$$-$$$: all major credit cards accepted
dinner. reservations recommended

minneapolis: north loop / warehouse >

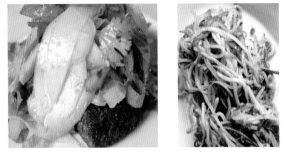

112 Eatery has become such an essential place to eat in the Twin Cities that without it, these cities would be like *Sex and the City* with no Carrie, *American Idol* with no Simon, Captain with no Tennille. In other words, things would just not be the same, or as delicious, without *112 Eatery*. But with adoration comes a downside, which means having to sometimes wait in line for a table. But it's an easy guarantee to make that once you get yourself that comfortable seat and you're eating this divine food, you'll be as happy as Carrie in a shoe store.

imbibe / devour:
08 punto final mendoza malbec
08 lioco rosé
sweet & sour crab salad
lamb scottadito with goat's milk yogurt
bacon egg & harissa sandwich
buttermilk fried chicken with bagna cauda
chinese fried eggs
nancy silverton's butterscotch budino

a baker's wife pastry shop

baked goods that could make you cry
4200 28th avenue south. corner of 42nd
612.729.6898
tue - sat 6:30a - 6p sun 6:30a - 3p

opened in 1987. owner: gary tolle
$: cash only
treats. first come, first served

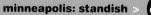 **minneapolis: standish >** **e02**

PLAIN-OR-
CIN. SUGAR
DONUTS
¢.47

The American teacake might conjure up something like this: a dainty confection that you would nibble at during afternoon tea while gingerly sipping black tea with your pinky pointing. Get this imagery out of your head as it's wrong, wrong, wrong. The American teacake is anything but dainty. It is sweet and crunchy, sticky and chewy, caramelized and crispy and ginormous. And where does one find this behemoth? At *A Baker's Wife Pastry Shop*, where it's just one of the many ridiculously delicious pastries on offer. This darn teacake makes me proud to be an American.

imbibe / devour:
cinnamon sugar cake
american tea cake
sour cherry danish
cinnamon bread
crème brûlée danish
chocolate cookie
cake doughnuts
pain au chocolat

MILK

abu nader

middle eastern deli and grocery

2095 como avenue. corner of raymond
651.647.5391 www.abunaderdeli.com
mon - sat 11a - 8p

opened in 1999. owner: bishara ailabouni
$: visa. mc
lunch. dinner. deli. grocery. first come, first served

st paul: st anthony park >

The thing about pictures of food is that even though we might not realize it, people want food pictures to look, well, prettier than the food often is. Cue food stylists. At *eat.shop* we shoot the food exactly as it's served—no primping, no spritzing. If the food looks good in these pictures, then it is, like the gorgeous falafel sandwich at *Abu Nader*. Although it's hard to imagine any sandwich could arrive so overflowing and jam-packed full, this is, in fact, exactly how it's made. A downside? This monster is easier to shoot than to eat, but I managed to do so without leaving so much as a morsel behind.

imbibe / devour:
arabic coffee
spinach pie
pepper & feta pie
grape leaves
falafel sandwich
shawarma
baklava
knafeh

bar la grassa

authentic italian pasta

800 washington avenue north. between eighth and ninth
612.333.3837 www.barlagrassa.com twitter: @barlagrassa
mon - thu 5p - midnight fri - sat 5p - 1a sun 5p - midnight

opened in 2009. owner / chef: isaac becker owner: nancy st. pierre
$$-$$$: all major credit cards accepted
dinner. reservations accepted

minneapolis: north loop / warehouse >

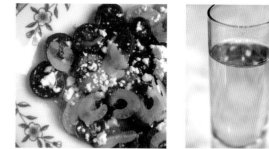

For years I have said that I was going to make pasta. I have printed out recipes, read extensively on techniques and researched pasta-making machines and equipment. And I have, as yet, to press out a single orecchiette. It's time for me to face the facts: I'm never going to make my own pasta. Instead I will happily eat at *Bar La Grassa,* which serves up fresh pasta so deliciously supple it makes me wonder why I would ever consider DIY noodles when I can just eat here and reap the benefits. Just be sure to actually save room for the pasta after you've made it through the I-have-to-try-each-one list of bruschetta.

imbibe / devour:
housemade limoncello
04 vino nobile sangiovese / merlot
taleggio bigne with braised apple
soft eggs & lobster bruschetta
red wine spaghetti with pine nuts
burrata & chili bruschetta
fresh gnocchi with cauliflower & orange
porchetta

barbette

bistroesque dining

1600 west lake street. corner of irving avenue
612.827.5710 www.barbette.com twitter: @barbettempls
sun - thu 8a - 1a fri - sat 8a - 2a

opened in 2001. owner: kim bartmann chef: kevin kathman
$$: all major credit cards accepted
breakfast. lunch. dinner. reservations accepted

minneapolis: uptown >

Once upon a time, many years ago, I was in Paris with my family and we found ourselves without a good restaurant recommendation. The situation got worse as the night wore on, and finally we ended up in a terrible Chinese restaurant. When I think back, what we were looking for was a place like *Barbette*. A cozy spot with an old-fashioned feel for steak frites, salade niçoise and something delicious to drink. Though Paris is nice, I'll take *Barbette,* in the glamorous Twin Cities, over a mediocre meal in the City of Lights anytime.

imbibe / devour:
pimms cup
house red
croque monsieur
chef's buckwheat crepe
warm duck confit salad
brandade fritter
steak au poivre
chocolate cake

birchwood cafe

cozy neighborhood cafe

3311 east 25th street. corner of 33rd
612.722.4474 www.birchwoodcafe.com twitter: @birchwoodcafe
mon - fri 7a - 10p sat 8a - 10p sun 9a - 8p

opened in 1995. owner: tracy singleton chef: marshall paulsen
$-$$: visa. mc
breakfast. lunch. dinner. first come, first served

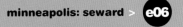

minneapolis: seward > **e06**

I travel a lot for my job, and I have fine-tuned my packing to include a small suitcase of accoutrements and travel necessities. It would be nice, however, to be able to pack a consistent, delicious place to eat like *Birchwood Café*. Although I've had an amazing number of delicious meals in my travels, I often find myself in need of a hearty, homey nutritious one, someplace that would make me feel like I'm at my mom's table, and not on the road. *Birchwood* hits these notes for me. If it only came in a 3 oz. travel-size container, life would be perfect.

imbibe / devour:
victory prime pils
bell's two-hearted ale
pumpkin & vegetable handpie
savory waffle
quiche du jour
ham & cheese melt
cherry raspberry maple crisp
ice cream float

blackbird*

casual, classic cafe

815 west 50th street. between bryant and aldrich
612.823.4790 www.blackbirdmpls.com
mon - fri 11a - 9p sat 8a - 10p sun 8a - 2p

opened in 2007. owner / chef: chris stevens
$$: visa. mc
breakfast. lunch. dinner. reservations accepted
*please check website to see if blackbird has re-opened

minneapolis: tangletown >

I was reading *Blackbird's* website and I couldn't help but think the copy sounded like a really compelling personal ad of someone I'd totally want to date: Casually classic. Whimsically alluring. Charmingly snuggly. Though I'm already spoken for, this sounds much better than "Everybody says I look like Brad Pitt." While I'm not in the dating scene, I am in the dining scene, and I do look for the above attributes when eating out. In short, a place that is comfortable, with enough charm to keep me interested, and a menu that is, well, casually classic. I believe I have found my restaurant soul mate.

imbibe / devour:
06 lang & reed cabernet franc
old rasputin imperial russian stout
butterhead salad
tomato basil soup
tea-smoked salmon
hoisin pulled-pork sandwich
bbq babyback ribs
carrot cake

black sheep

coal-fired pizza

600 washington avenue north. corner of sixth
612.342.2625 www.blacksheeppizza.com
sun - thu 11:30a - 10p fri - sat 11:30a - 11p

opened in 2008. owner: jordan smith
$$: all major credit cards accepted
dinner. reservations accepted

minneapolis: north loop / warehouse >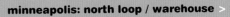

I get excited when people are able to bring something new to the table, both literally and figuratively in this case. While coal fire isn't new by any means, *Black Sheep Coal Fire Pizza* is the first I've happened upon that is baked by coal fire. In a world of wood-burning, brick pizza ovens, this is exciting to a pizza geek like me. And once I tasted the pie here, I kept coming back and back and back again. For now, this may be a one-of-a-kind spot, but I would bet a chicken and pickled pepper pizza that the copy cats are coming. Good luck to them, as the bar is set high by this savory spot.

imbibe / devour:
surly furious
black sheep house red or white
spinach blue cheese salad
pizza:
  tomato & oregano
  hot salami & dried chili pepper
  oyster mushroom, smoked mozzarella
    & rosemary

brasa

premium rotisserie

m: east hennepin avenue. corner of sixth
sp: 777 grand avenue. between grotto and avon
612.397.3030 www.brasa.us twitter: @brasarotisserie
see website for hours

opened in 2007. owner / chef: alexander roberts
$-$$: all major credit cards accepted
lunch. dinner. first come, first served

minneapolis: northeast > 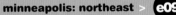 **e09**

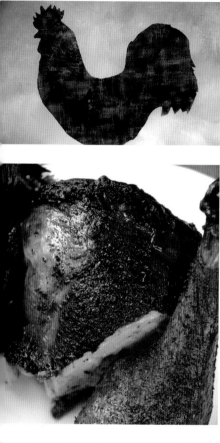

Creating an *eat.shop* guide is a bit like running a marathon, what with the nonstop eating and shopping and eating again and eating yet again. This doesn't stop until the book is fully researched and in the bag. In the middle of this event, there is always a place where I hit my stride, get my second wind, and feel a rush of euphoria to finish the final leg. *Brasa* was my euphoric moment during this book as I sat with my husband outside here on a warm evening, devouring plates of pulled pork, rotisserie chicken and delicious sides. It was like I hadn't had a bite to eat in weeks.

imbibe / devour:
draft beers: surly, bells
mexican coke
rotisserie chicken
roasted pork sandwich
warm cornbread with honey butter
yams & andouille
crispy yuca with mojo
banana pudding

bryant lake bowl

all day dining and bowling

810 west lake street. corner of bryant
612.825.3737 www.bryantlakebowl.com twitter: @bryantlakebowl
daily 8a - 2a

opened in 1993. owners: the bartmann family chef: al potyondy-smith
$$: all major credit cards accepted
breakfast. lunch. dinner. bowling. first come, first served

minneapolis: uptown > 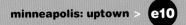 **e10**

Things got a little tricky for me at *Bryant Lake Bowl* because I needed a bit of a refresher course on how to keep score by hand. I've gotten spoiled by the new-fangled electronic scorekeepers. Luckily it all came back to me, though I guess it didn't matter as I was missing most of the pins anyway. I took comfort that the menu here didn't confuse me in the least and it's chock full of strikes—the ordering was like bowling with bumpers. Though this blurb is full of bowling clichés, the food and atmosphere here is truly original.

imbibe / devour:
lagunitas lil sumpin extra
bells double cream stout
sunnyside hash & eggs
smoked trout & roasted beet salad
pulled pastures a plenty pork sandwich
spicy black bean burger
pan-fried sunfish
cheesecake

cafe levain

neighborhood french bistro

4762 chicago avenue south. between 47th and 48th

612.823.7111 www.cafelevain.com

tue - thu 5 - 9p fri - sat 5 - 10p sun 5 - 9p

opened in 2007. owner: harvey mclain

$$: all major credit cards accepted

dinner. reservations accepted

minneapolis: south > **e11**

I'm acutely aware of trends in food because I eat at so many places across the country. One of 2009's biggest trends? The sunny side up egg on top of anything and everything. I was getting really tired of this trick until I visited *Cafe Levain*. Never before have I wanted to eat an egg so badly. This orb was perfectly poached, just-broken and oozing over a fat meat patty, topped with caramelized onions and cornichons creating a monster burger. Holy clucker. Yes, the burger at *Cafe Levain* may well be a star, but I think the egg stole the show.

imbibe / devour:
sunday suppers
french onion soup
thousand hills grass-fed burger
braised beef short rib
tasmanian ocean trout
pearl barley risotto
banana split
choclate truffle torte

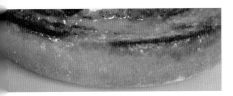

colossal cafe

american scratch cookin'

1839 east 42nd street. between cedar and longfellow
612.729.2377 www.colossalcafe.com
wed - sun 6a - 3p

opened in 2005. owner / chef: bess giannakakis
$-$$: cash only
breakfast. lunch. first come, first served

minneapolis: powderhorn > 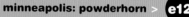 **e12**

Every year my brother-in-law bakes something divine on Christmas morning. Sometimes it's a sticky bun, sometimes it's a biscuit—but no matter what, it's always delicious. Lately David's baked goods have (almost) been outshining my mom's beloved annual breakfast dish. I feel the same excitement I have for David's baked creations when I come to *Colossal Café*. Chunky scones and fat cookies, the homemade biscuits used for the egg sandwiches, the famous flips. All the flour-based edibles in this small, skinny café are a big fat success. Colossal, if you will.

imbibe / devour:
coffee
iced tea
homemade buttermilk biscuit
flip-house pastry specialty
egg, cheddar & bacon sandwich
apple, walnut & brie flappers
veggie melt sandwich
spiced turkey sandwich

el burrito mercado

mexican market, restaurant and deli
175 cesar chavez street. corner of state street
651.227.2192 www.elburritomercado.com
daily 7a - 8p

opened in 1979. owners: tomas and maria silva
$: all major credit cards accepted
breakfast. lunch. dinner. grocery. first come, first served

st. paul: west side > 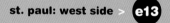 **e13**

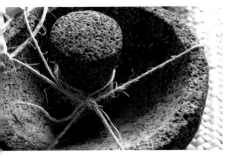

When I was a kid, I always took a packed lunch to school. Occasionally, however, the cafeteria offerings made me want to ditch my home-packed meal, like on the Mexican-themed days with churros as dessert. Looking back I realize those churros weren't so hot, but that hasn't dampened my love for them. Despite drooling over the hot fried cinnamon dough at *El Burrito Mercado*, I amazingly did NOT get one the last time I ate here because I was so stuffed with the guisado platter that even I, dedicated churro fanatic, didn't have an inch to spare.

imbibe / devour:
limon jarritos
mexican hot chocolate
chile relleno
chicken mole
carne al pastor taco taco
chimichangas
burrito original
churros

golden fig fine foods

a grocery filled with locally produced foods

790 grand avenue. between avon and grotto
651.602.0144 www.goldenfig.com twitter: @goldenfig
see website for hours

opened in 2006. owner: laurie mccann crowell
$: all major credit cards accepted
grocery. first come, first served

st paul: grand avenue >

It's a fantasy of mine to leave the city, divest myself of all wordly possessions (okay, well, most of them) and buy a farm. My vision includes fresh eggs from laying hens, an organic vegetable garden and a fat mama pig with a pile of piglets—you know, it's the living with the land and breathing fresh air type o' fantasy. Until this dream becomes a reality, I plan to live vicariously through those who are already living it and selling their wares to *Golden Fig*. This place is chock-full of locally made or farmer-produced goods. I feel happier already knowing that there's a place where I can at least feed my fantasy.

imbibe / devour:
free-range chickens & eggs
thousand hills grass-fed beef
butter almond toffee
golden fig sun-dried tomato dill dip packet
rockstar dill pickle seeds
csabai hungarian salami
nutorious chipotle nuts
berry bliss bark

heidi's*

intimate, fine dining
819 west 50th street. between bryant and aldrich
612.354.3512 www.heidismpls.com
tue - thu 5 - 9p fri - sat 5 - 10p

opened in 2007
owner / chef: stewart woodman owners: heidi woodman and frank thorpe
$$-$$$: all major credit cards accepted
dinner. reservations accepted
*please check website to see if heidi's has re-opened

minneapolis: tangletown > **e15**

I don't know about you, but I'm flummoxed by all the user-reviewed restaurant apps and websites out there. Half of the people are madly in love with a place and the other half are venting about their terrible service and horrible food. It's like the U.S. Senate—nobody can agree. *Heidi's*, however, is a different story. Everyone loves *Heidi's*. Everyone. And they're all out there in virtual land spouting their affection. Why the unanimous bliss? Because this place is romantic and intimate, the food is creative and fun and mind blowingly delicious. See people, you can actually agree on something.

imbibe / devour:
05 bodegas mustiguillo mestizaje bobal
crispin cocktail
lobster bisque
soft poached hen egg
australian sea bass
sesame crusted rainbow trout
anise scented lamb shank
banana napoleon

isles bun & coffee

enormous, delicious baked buns

1424 west 28th street. corner of hennepin
612.870.4466 www.islesbun.com twitter: @islesbun
mon - sat 6:30a - 4p sun 7a - 3p

opened in 1993. owners: jeff and catherine veigel
$: all major credit cards accepted
treats. first come, first served

minneapolis: uptown > 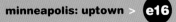e16

I think it's a good sign when the equipment used to make an oversized sticky bun is made by the same manufacturers who are known for serious machinery, John Deere in this case. Obviously *Isles's* buns won't be described with these adjectives: petite, delicate or light, but these descriptors do apply: hefty, hearty, sticky, gooey. If you are a wimpy bun eater, bring a friend to share one of the big ones or get a puppy dog tail. Because I am not a wimpy bun eater (and have my own bun in the oven to feed), I swiftly devoured every doughy bite of goodness.

imbibe / devour:
isles blend coffee
hot chocolate
puppy dog tails
cinnamon buns
caramel sticky buns
caramel pecan buns
biscotti
coffee cake

izzy's ice cream cafe

homemade artisan ice cream

2034 marshall avenue. between cleveland and wilder
651.603.1458 www.izzysicecream.com twitter: @izzysicecream
mon - thu 3 - 9p fri - sat 1 - 10p sun 1 - 9p

opened in 2000. owners: lara hammel and jeff sommers
$: all major credit cards accepted
treats. first come, first served

st paul: merriam park > 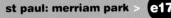 **e17**

The creator of *eat.shop,* Kaie, oftens says that the businesses we feature in these books are the kind you would drive across town in rush-hour traffic to get to. I would like to add in *Izzy's* case that I had such an intense urge for their ice cream that I drove not only in rush hour traffic, but for added fun, in the first snow of the season, which was coming down wet and thick. I was kind of glad it took awhile because it gave me time to think about my choices: A banana split? A scoop of Oreo and/or mint chocolate chip? A snowstorm and gridlock is no match for my love of *Izzy's.*

imbibe / devour:
ice cream:
   cinnamon
   hot brown sugar
   italian strawberry
   tiramisu
   salted caramel
   peppermint bon bon
   peace coffee

jasmine deli

beloved vietnamese deli

2532 nicollet avenue south. between 25th and 26th
612.870.4700
tue - sun 10a - 8p sun 10a - 6p

opened in 2001. owner / chef: vinh truong
$: cash only
lunch. dinner. first come, first served

minneapolis: whittier > 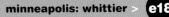 **e18**

Though it's been said it couldn't be done, I've found a cure for the common cold, and because I'm a generous soul, I am going to share the cure with you. It's the pho at *Jasmine Deli*. While hot broth is nothing new to comforting a runny nose, this pho doesn't just soothe folks, it cures. The bit of heat from the fresh jalapeño, and the massive bowl of broth and noodles that pulls you into a trance of slurping scientifically eliminates sniffles and sneezes. Having declared myself both researcher and doctor, my pronouncement is that this pho is one medicine that works.

imbibe / devour:
vietnamese coffee
coconut bubble tea
bún nuoc
bánh mì
spring rolls
stir-fried vermicelli noodle salad
broken rice pork chop plate

43

kopplin's

really good coffee

490 hamline avenue south. between randolph and juno
651.698.0457 www.kopplinscoffee.com twitter: @kopplins
mon 6a - 4p tue - fri 6a - 8p sat - sun 7a - 8p

opened in 2006. owner: andrew kopplin
$: visa. mc
coffee. treats. first come, first served

st. paul: mac-groveland > e19

There are three things that are top of my list after I have my baby: take a scalding hot bath, eat a plate full of raw fish and drink cup after cup of *Kopplin's* coffee. Andrew has a reputation in the Twin Cities for making the best cuppa joe in town—I could barely contain myself from indulging here while watching happy caffeinites start their day right. If coffee doesn't rock your boat, the tea selection here is just as carefully curated—though I will say to you tea people, I think you are missing out. *Kopplin's* might have you switching teams, if you give it a chance.

imbibe / devour:
espresso
cafe miel
chai of the month
cold press coffee
rogue hot chocolate
bostock
danish
rustic cookie

la belle vie

exquisite cocktails and fine food

510 groveland avenue. at hennepin
612.874.6440 www.labellevie.us
mon - thu 5 - 9p fri - sat 5 - 10p sun 5 - 9p

opened in 1998. owner / chef: tim mckee
owners: bill summerville and josh thoma
$$$: all major credit cards accepted
dinner. reservations recommended

minneapolis: loring park > e20

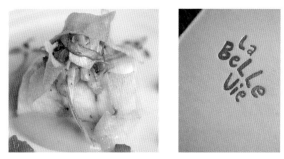

My husband and I went to *La Belle Vie* with the intention of having dessert. It was 10 pm, so we had already eaten dinner. But once we settled in the cozy, romantic lounge, we somehow got sidetracked from our original plan. First we ordered drinks, then we decided we needed truffled fries to accompany them. Soon a plate of rabbit pappardelle was ordered and devoured, and it took quite a bit of convincing to get Shawn not to order a second plate (he's still reminding me of this). This is the sort of seductive place where good intentions might go by the wayside, but that's not a bad thing.

imbibe / devour:
cortez the killer cocktail
we choose to go to the moon cocktail
housemade potato chips with truffle sauce
pappardelle with rabbit bolognese & porcini
quail with mustard, rapini & smoked paprika
vanilla poached persimmons
peanut butter bread pudding with
  manjari ice cream

la chaya bistro

mexican-italian bistro

4537 nicollet avenue south. between 45th and 46th
612.827.2254 www.lachaya.com
mon - sat lunch 11a - 3p dinner 5 - 11p

opened in 2008. owner / chef: juan garcia owner: dave kopfmann
$$-$$$: all major credit cards accepted
lunch. dinner. brunch. reservations accepted

minneapolis: kingfield > e21

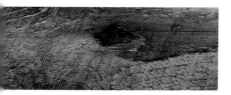

Word-of-mouth gushing is essential to my job, meaning almost everybody I meet loves to share with me their favorite spots. But at the end of the day, I still have to vet everything to see what works for *eat. shop*. Far and away the best suggestion I received for this book was from Scott at *Tangletown Gardens* who insisted I visit *La Chaya*. As I continued to work on the book, the *La Chaya* recs multiplied. So I visited. The innovative approach (Mexican and Italian?!) here is fresh, totally homey and delicious. So I will add my voice to the waterfall of gushes.

imbibe / devour:
michelada
dos equis
tacos de pescado
molletes con chorizo
achiote rubbed chicken sandwich
white pizza with garlic, rosemary & olive oil
housemade cannelloni
coriander crusted halibut over mashed potato

lucia's to go

exceptionally good take out

1432 west 31st street. between hennepin and holmes
612.825.9800 www.lucias.com
tue - fri 7a - 8p sat 8a - 8p sun 8a - 5p

opened in 2006. owner / chef: lucia watson
$-$$: all major credit cards accepted
breakfast. lunch. dinner. treats. first come, first served

minneapolis: uptown >

While thinking about names for my unborn baby, I got thinking about how people choose baby names. There's the family name of course, or the name you've dreamt of calling your child since you were 11 (you might want to rethink Sparrow Midnight as it's been taken). I'm thinking if I have a daughter, I might call her Lucia, so she would be inspired by the owner who loves all things fresh and local or inclined to bake treats like the ones you can find at *Lucia's To Go*. Who wouldn't want his/her child to be able to bake chocolate chip cookies like the ones you can find here?

imbibe / devour:
cafe latte
chai latte
berry butter crêpe
daily frittata
spinach walnut pesto pasta salad
pear apple arugula salad
lori callister free-range chicken salad
fresh baked breads!

maria's cafe

a fusion of north and south america cuisines

1113 east franklin avenue. corner of 11th
612.870.9842 www.mariascafe.com
mon - sat 7a - 3p sun 8a - 3p

opened in 1998. owner / chef: maria hoyos
$-$$: all major credit cards accepted
breakfast. lunch. first come, first served

minneapolis: midtown / phillips > **e23**

We live in a world of hype and spin these days, so it's pretty hard to know when something is the real deal. For example, there's a fair amount of hype regarding the corn pancakes at *Maria's Cafe*. Because it's my job to cast a critical eye, I wasn't going to pass judgment until the first bite. Yum. Yum yum yum. This pancake is moist, sweet with the taste of corn and equally as good doused in syrup or smothered with cheese. I plotted how I could eat them for breakfast, lunch and dinner. So yes, do believe the hype to which I'm now adding.

imbibe / devour:
guava juice
house-blend colombian coffee
cachapas venezolanas (corn pancakes)
pablo's omelet
maria's colombian huevos pericos
giovanni's breakfast wrap
raisin bran muffin
guava turnover

mill city cafe

eclectic eating establishment
2205 california street northeast. corner of 22nd
612.788.6188 www.millcitycafe.com
tue - fri 8a - 3p sat - sun 9a - 2p

opened in 2005. owner: mandy zechmeister
$-$$: all major credit cards accepted
lunch. brunch. first come, first served

minneapolis: northeast >

As I was eating my breakfast at *Mill City Cafe*, I noticed a couple of men in bright orange vests enjoying a snack and coffee over by the bar. They stood the whole time and walked out a few minutes before I did. As I was getting in my car, I heard a loud train whistle and looked up to see the two men pulling away in the train they had left "parked" on the tracks. You've got to love this about *Mill City Cafe*—it's the type of nestled little eating spot that draws people from all parts of town via all modes of transport. Have train, will travel.

imbibe / devour:
fresh-squeezed orange juice
cinnamon wild rice pancakes
chorizo breakfast burrito
mexican baked eggs
mill mac burger
baby blue burger
northeast cuban sandwich
mac & cheese

modern café

the place you want to eat

337 13th avenue northeast. between university and fourth
612.378.9882 www.moderncafeminneapolis.com
tue - thu 11a - 9p fri 11a - 9:30p sat 8a - 9:30p sun 8a - 2p

opened in 1994. owner: jim grell chef: philip becht
$$: visa. mc
breakfast. lunch. dinner. first come, first served

minneapolis: northeast > 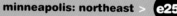 **e25**

I tend to be an indecisive person about a multitude of things. For my personal style, I veer between classic and clean or messy and a little boho. My home is modern and sparse, but I am sometimes attracted to the cluttered vintage look. The one area of my life that I'm crystal clear on is my taste in restaurants, and *Modern Café* is precisely, exactly my type. This is the type of spot I want to eat at any day of the week, and there's nothing that could change my mind on that. Now if I could only decide on what to eat here. Will it be the mac and cheese, or the grilled cheese sandwich?

imbibe / devour:
summit extra pale ale
tortoise creek pinot noir
duck paté
pork & cabbage pancakes
stewed chickpeas
lamb burger
modern hash
berkshire osso buco

moto-i

the first sake brewery restaurant outside of japan

2940 south lyndale avenue. between lake and 28th
612.821.6262 www.moto-i.com
daily noon - 2a

opened in 2008. owner: blake richardson chef: jason engelhart
$$: all major credit cards accepted
lunch. dinner. reservations accepted

minneapolis: uptown > e26

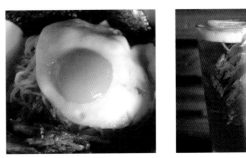

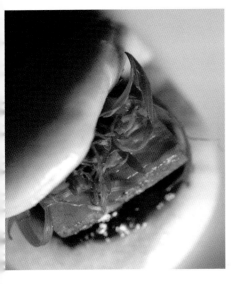

It's my job to talk about the food at the restaurants I like, and I have every intention of talking about the food here at *Moto-i*. But I have to talk first about table shuffleboard. I didn't know how much fun it was until I played it here. I mean, it's really entertaining. Yes, *Moto-i* is uber cool and yes, this is the first sake brewery restaurant outside of Japan, and yes the Japanese style pub grub goes down well with the sake BUT after you've eaten, do you want to play a game of shuffleboard with me?? I'd like to challenge you to a match. The sake is on me.

imbibe / devour:
nama nectar
sake flights
fried shishito peppers
house-cured kimchee & pickles
thai beef jerky
pork dumplings
sata andagi
daily ice cream with sweet potato candy

pizza nea

neapolitan pizza

306 east hennepin avenue. between university and fifth
612.331.9298 www.pizzanea.com
mon - thu 11a - 9:30p fri - sat 11a - 10:30p sun noon - 9p

opened in 2003. owner: mike sherwood
$$: visa. mc
lunch. dinner. first come, first served

minneapolis: northeast > **e27**

From the simple to the sublime, we all have foods that trigger a Proustian memory. Here's a few of mine: saltine crackers and ginger ale=staying home from school when sick. Flank steak and broiled tomatoes=mom's home cooking. Thin margherita pizza=my year spent living in Rome. We often forget the foods that spike pleasant memories, but now that I know *Pizza Nea* will shoot me directly to that feeling of being at a Roman pizzeria, it's hard to stay away. With or without a déjà vu moment, this pizza will take you someplace else altogether.

imbibe / devour:
peroni
bruschetta
polpette napoletane
caprese salad
pizzas:
  spinaci
  diavola
  quattro stagione

quang

family owned vietnamese restaurant
2719 nicollet avenue. between 27th and 28th
www.quangrestaurant.com
mon 11a - 9p wed - fri 11a - 9p sat 10a - 9p sun 10a - 8:30p

opened in 1989. owner: mrs. quang
$$: all major credit cards accepted
lunch. dinner. first come, first served

minneapolis: whittier >

Sometimes a city will have a longstanding eatery that is so beloved and well-known, it doesn't feel like it needs any more press. *Quang* falls into this category; hence why it wasn't in the first edition of this book. But when putting together the second edition, I couldn't shake the feeling that *Quang* is so much a part of the food vernacular in this city that it isn't right not to feature it. So for those of you who know and love *Quang*, count this as your reminder to go again soon. And if you are a visitor to the Twin Cities, this legendary Vietnamese spot is not to be missed!

imbibe / devour:
vietnamese iced coffee
soya bean drink
fresh spring rolls
fresh-sliced beef noodle soup
ground sugarcane shrimp over rice noodles
stir-fried jumbo shrimp, onions & bean sprouts
mochi dumplings
baked coconut sweet bread

red stag supperclub

eco-friendly lodge meets divine cooking

509 first avenue northeast. between fifth and sixth

www.redstagsupperclub.com

mon - fri 11a - 2a sat - sun 9a - 2a

opened in 2007. owner: kim bartmann chef: brian hauke

$$: all major credit cards accepted

lunch. dinner. brunch. reservations accepted

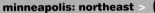 **minneapolis: northeast >** **e29**

Do you ever contemplate moving out of the city, up north to the woods where you have to snowshoe, cross-country ski or snow mobile to get around and where roaring fires are the only way you ever get really warm? I imagine a place like *Red Stag Supper Club* would be the central meeting spot where you'd share a beer with your pals, a heaping pile of French fries and a hearty slab of a roast. Though I love this vision, *Red Stag* is so much better in reality because you don't have to hike 10 miles in waist-deep snow to get to it. There are benefits to living in civilization.

imbibe / devour:
tripel karmeliet
bells best brown ale
relish plate
minnesota milled grits
brick pressed chicken
elk stroganoff
lamb duo
pan-roasted duck

rustica bakery

addictively delicious baked goods

3224 west lake street. between calhoun and chowen
612.822.1119 www.rusticabakery.com
mon - fri 6:30a - 8p sat - sun 7a - 8p

opened in 2004. owners: stephen horton and barbara shaterian
$: visa. mc
treats. first come, first served

minneapolis: calhoun village > 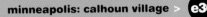 **e30**

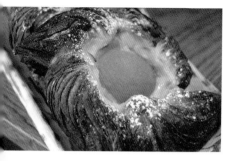

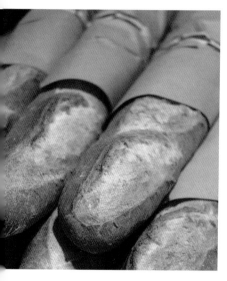

What's up with people shunning the bread basket? Carb terror is so five years ago. I would never turn down a bread basket, especially in this town, as chances are the contents are coming from *Rustica Bakery*. I can't get within five miles of this place without making a stop for a warm treat. Even if I were to try to test the limits of my temptation by waving off the basket, I'd be immediately plunged into fantasies of *Rustica's* baguettes, with their crunchy crusts and soft insides. I'd be chasing down the waitress, pleading to have the basket back. This is what *Rustica's* breads and baked goods will reduce you to.

imbibe / devour:
baguette
focaccia
olive bread
egg braid
currant rye
zucchero cookie
bittersweet chocolate cookie
bostok

salty tart

hidden gem of a bakery

920 east lake street. in midtown global market
612.874.9206 www.saltytart.com
mon - sat 7a - 8p sun 9a - 6p

opened in 2008. owner: michelle gayer
$: visa. mc
treats. first come, first served

minneapolis: midtown / phillips > **e31**

At first glance, the quiet little storefront of the *Salty Tart* could go unnoticed. There's something about this place that feels like it would fit perfectly on the Left Bank in Paris. It's the type of spot to press your nose against the window and watch as the busy bakers pull warm loaves from the oven and roll pastry dough thin. I found myself momentarily transfixed by my Paris fantasy until I looked around and was transported back to the Midtown Market, with its myriad of shops and eateries. I wasn't disappointed though, because I knew when I entered here, there was a treasure (or two or three) awaiting me.

imbibe / devour:
pastry cream-filled brioche
chocolate cupcake
sweet scone
peanut butter whole wheat cookie
ginger sugar cookie
oatmeal chocolate sour cherry cookie
sweet turnover
sourdough bread

69

sen yai sen lek

thai rice and noodles

2422 central avenue northeast. between lowry and 24th
612.781.3046 www.senyai-senlek.com
mon - thu 11a - 9p fri - sat 11a - 10p

opened in 2008. owner / chef: joe hatch-surisook owner: holly hatch-surisook
$$: visa. mc
lunch. dinner. deli. grocery. first come, first served

minneapolis: northeast > **e32**

Despite some clichéd stereotypes, Minneapolis is not solely populated by hardy folk who spend their days eating *vörtbröd* and fishing for *lutefisk*. There's also an enormous Thai population and, with that, some of the best Thai food you'll eat in this country. Anyone who lives in Minneapolis knows this already, but for visitors this can be a surprise. And where's a great spot to get amazing Thai food? *Sen Yai Sen Lek*, where the word delicious can be attributed to every dish in the house, including a Tom Yum soup that will visit me often in my dreams.

imbibe / devour:
flat earth xanadu
singha lager
pad bpai gra pow
po pia tod
som tum
pad see iew gai
khao newo mamuang
gluay buad chee

sugar sugar

divine candy shop

3803 grand avenue south. between 38th and 39th
612.823.0261 www.sugar-sugarcandy.com
tue - sat 11a - 7p sun noon - 5p

opened in 2009. owner: joni wheeler
$: all credit cards accepted
treats. first come, first served

minneapolis: uptown > **s33**

You know the moment in *The Wizard of Oz* when Dorothy drops into Oz and everything turns to color? This is what you'll experience when you enter *Sugar Sugar*: Technicolor explosion—it's as though you've been living in black and white without having a clue about your colorless existence. This colororama is thanks to Joni's acute attention to detail, from the chocolate wrappers she finds in France to the vintage candy boxes she collects and displays on her walls to the actual candy itself which will make you smile like the proverbial kid in a candy store.

devour:
papabubble candy rings
oliver kita chocolate buddha
maison bouche lavender bar
rogue chocolate raw chocolate
fine & raw chocolate
payard chocolate perfume
french macaroons
organic gummy bears

sweets bakeshop

baked delights

2042 marshall avenue. between cleveland and wilder
651.340.7138 www.ssweetsstudio.com
tue - sun 11a - 6p

opened in 2009. owners: ly lo and krista steinbach
$-$$: all major credit cards accepted
treats. first come, first served

st paul: merriam park >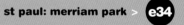

I think it's sweet when people renew their wedding vows, though it's never been something I imagined for myself. Until now. And I'll fess up, the only reason I'm reconsidering is because I want a full-blown dessert table created by *Sweets Bakeshop*. Though I don't think we have anything new to say in the vows department, I'll think of something to say if we can have an *SS* wedding cake, big platters of cookies and white chocolate covered marshmallows. What's my husband think about all this? I'm just going to give him a cupcake from here, and that should help him see the light.

imbibe / devour:
daily cupcakes
brownies & blondies
french macaroons
white chocolate-covered marshmallows
custom:
  cupcakes
  cakes
  dessert tables

the anchor fish & chips

really delicious fish & chips

302 13th avenue northeast. between third and university
612.676.1300 www.theanchorfishandchips.com
tue - fri 4p - 1a sat - sun 10a - 1a

opened in 2009. owners: kathryn hayes, luke kyle and jenny crouser
$-$$: visa. mc
lunch. dinner. breakfast. first come, first served

minneapolis: northeast >

The Anchor
Fish & Chips

The last time I remember enjoying fish and chips as much as the ones at *The Anchor*, I was in the motherland (London, England). I had arrived in the city and found my room not ready (argh), so I was kicked out onto the streets exhausted, dirty and supremely grumpy. I eventually found myself at a little pub that produced the perfect plate of fish and chips, and I was grumpy no more. This memory came flooding back to me at *The Anchor*. And though this time I had no grumps to cure, I head the same overwhelming sense of pleasure after eating. Fish and chips are good for you.

imbibe / devour:
guinness
harp
fish & chips
pastie & chips
shepherd's pie
battered sausage
mushy peas
curry chips

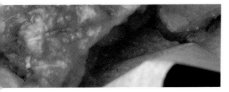

the blue door pub

home of the juicy blucy
1811 selby avenue. between fairview and wheeler
651.493.1865 www.thebdp.com
sun - sat 11a - 1a

opened in 2008. owners: jeremy woerner and patrick mcdonough
$-$$: all major credit cards accepted
breakfast. lunch. dinner. first come, first served

st paul: merriam park > 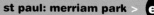 **e36**

There is an argument to be made that classics are best left alone i.e., the Juicy Lucy at *Matt's Bar* (featured in the first edition). This is a classic, and there would be a revolt if the recipe ever changed. But if you believe a classic deserves some riffs, then try the Juicy Blucys at The *Blue Door Pub*. The entire menu here is made up of variations on the basic theme of patties filled with hot oozy cheese. These babies are so darn tasty and creative that it would be a shame to miss out on them. And though the burgers here are fancy, the place is a cozy haven. Settle in and devour.

imbibe / devour:
lift bridge farm girl
new holland
deep-fried pickles
tater tots
juicy blucys:
  the french
  cajun
  bacon

the craftsman

american restaurant and bar

4300 east lake street. corner of 43rd
612.722.0175 www.craftsmanrestaurant.com
sun - thu 4 - 9:30p fri - sat 4 - 10p brunch sun 10a - 3p

opened in 2004. owners: mike dooley and susan kennedy-dooley
chef: mike phillips
$$-$$$: all major credit cards accepted
dinner. brunch. reservations accepted

minneapolis: southeast >

American craftsman style, with origins in the British Arts and Crafts movement, came as a reaction to the Industrial Revolution, emphasizing hand-made over mass-produced, simplicity over opulence. This is what *The Craftsman*, the restaurant, is all about. The focus is local, organic, seasonal, simple and fresh. No unnecessary fuss, frill or ornament. The menus aren't overly chatty, the plates aren't overly adorned and the waiters don't ask you over and over again how your food is. This is dining in its purest form, and it's delicious. William Morris would be proud.

imbibe / devour:
stormy night cocktail
rocky's revenge brown ale
beet & chevre terrine with micro arugula
whole pancetta wrapped roasted trout
grilled red venison leg
cheddar, harissa & bacon beef burger
braised pulled pork sandwich with
  heirloom tomato preserves

the happy gnome

new american food with an enormous beer menu

498 selby avenue. between mackubin and western
651.287.2018 www.thehappygnome.com
mon - thu 11a - 1a fri - sat 11a - 2a sun 10a - 1a

opened in 2005. owner: nick miller chef: matthew hinman
$$-$$$: all major credit cards accepted
lunch. dinner. reservations accepted

st. paul: selby / dale >

Outside my window I can see an advertisement on the side of a building for some type of alcohol, with big letters that read "Bah, humbug!" So now I'm trying to avoid looking out that window because it's making me feel bah humbug-ish. If I just can't help myself, I'll avoid the bah humbugs altogether by going to *The Happy Gnome*. It's hard to be a Scrooge at this place, with its massive menu of ales and stouts, cozy booths and hefty game burgers. I do see some people here with dour faces, but I think they are just scowling at the Amish chicken.

imbibe / devour:
witkap pater dubbel
lift bridge farm girl saison
spicy green beans
buffalo wings
mn game burger
roasted butternut squash risotto
chili-basted amish half chicken
bison short ribs

the lexington

a st. paul landmark

1096 grand avenue. corner of lexington
651.222.5878 www.the-lexington.com
see website for hours

opened in 1935.   owner: tom scallen chef: chad white
$$-$$$: all major credit cards accepted
lunch. dinner. brunch. reservations accepted

st paul: grand avenue >

The Lexington is the human version of hibernating. There is essentially not a single window here. The chairs are comfy tufted leather, and deep enough that you might fall asleep after you sip your dry martini and devour your hearty pot pie. The bar is long and welcoming, and there always seems to be room for just one more to sidle up at it. This is the place to go when you need to be cocooned, a cave where you can eat and drink until you're finally ready to face the outdoors or daylight again, though neither might arrive before spring—so hunker down.

imbibe / devour:
classic martini
shrimp cocktail
onion rings
hot turkey sandwich
grilled clubhouse
chicken pot pie
housemade pot roast
new york strip steak

the strip club

meat and fish

378 north maria avenue. corner of sixth
651.793.6247 www.domeats.com
see website for hours

opened in 2008.   owner / chef: jd fratzke owners: tim niver and aaron johnson
$$-$$$: all major credit cards accepted
lunch. dinner. brunch. reservations accepted

st. paul: dayton's bluff >

I just read about a study that showed that cows with first names produce more milk. I'm guessing that cows with first names also taste better, and I'm thinking that maybe the cows found on the menu at *The Strip Club* had first names because, goodness, these steaks are realllly good. If the cows aren't what make this place great, then it's got to be the owners who were behind the revamped *Town Talk Diner*. Though they are no longer involved with *TTD*, you'll be the happier for it because they are putting all their considerable talents behind this place. That's good news.

imbibe / devour:
the jamo toe
chep puncha cocktail
grilled new york strip
walleye pie
ocean trout
meat on a stick
the devil's eggs
pig's eye poutine

two smart cookies

just-baked cookies

181 snelling avenue north. between dayton and selby
612.384.1069 www.smartcookieshop.com
mon - fri noon - 5:30p

opened in 2007. owners: patty mathews and melanie danke
$: all major credit cards accepted
treats. first come, first served

st. paul: snelling / hamline > **e41**

There are two things I tend to do when I am procrastinating: shower a lot and bake. So if you come to my house and I'm squeaky clean and smell of gingerbread, you'll know that I'm in the midst of missing deadlines. This is why I think *Two Smart Cookies* is a genius idea. Instead of obsessive showering, these two ladies are baking ridiculously delicious, hot-from-the-oven cookies that keep people coming back time after time. I'm thinking some long trips to *Two Smart Cookies* might be another great form of procrastination.

imbibe / devour:
cookies:
  snickerdoodle
  chai latte
  caramel chocolate chip
  chocolate chip
  triple ginger
  oatmeal raisin
  chocolate crinkle

minneapolis:
- ## northeast
  - ## audubon park

eat

shop

∧
NORTH

minneapolis:
north loop •
warehouse •

eat

e1 > 112 eatery
e5 > bar la grassa
e8 > black sheep

shop

s19 > kilroys
s22 > martin patrick 3
s23 > mitrebox

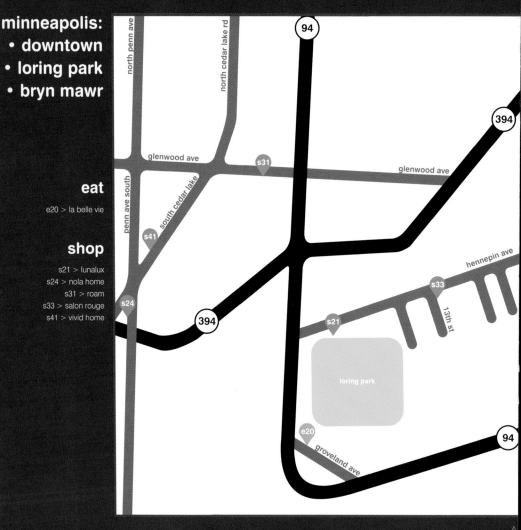

minneapolis:
- **downtown**
- **loring park**
- **bryn mawr**

eat

e20 > la belle vie

shop

s21 > lunalux
s24 > nola home
s31 > roam
s33 > salon rouge
s41 > vivid home

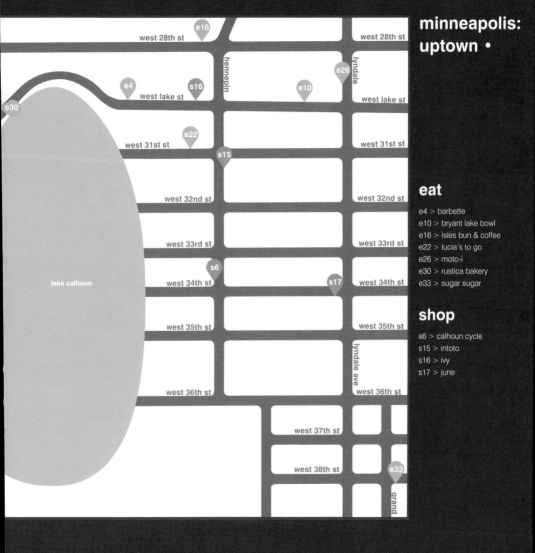

minneapolis:
uptown •

eat

e4 > barbette
e10 > bryant lake bowl
e16 > isles bun & coffee
e22 > lucia's to go
e26 > moto-i
e30 > rustica bakery
e33 > sugar sugar

shop

s6 > calhoun cycle
s15 > intoto
s16 > ivy
s17 > june

minneapolis:
- ## southwest
- ## linden hills
  - ## 50th and france

eat

shop

s4 > bluebird boutique
s5 > brown & greene
s8 > cooks of crocus hill
s11 > grethen house netc.
s12 > hunt & gather
s20 > ladyslipper boutique
s26 > oscar & belle
s32 > russell and hazel
s40 > victory
s42 > wonderment

france ave south

beard ave

xerxes ave

upton ave south

west 43rd

west 44th st

west 44th st

lake harriet

xerxes ave south

xerxes ave south

france ave south

west 50th st

west 50th st

NOR

minneapolis:
south •
tangletown •
kingfield •

eat

e7 > blackbird
e11 > cafe levain
e15 > heidi's
e21 > la chaya bistro

shop

s34 > shoppe local
s36 > style minneapolis
s37 > tangletown gardens

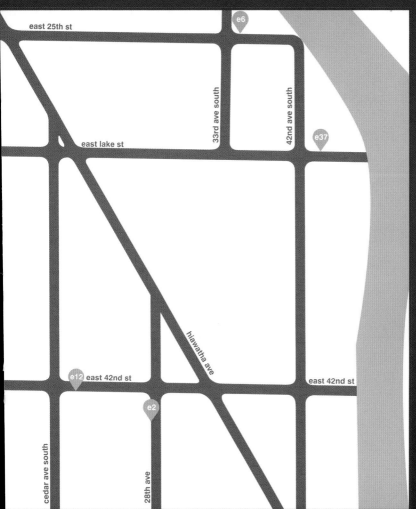

minneapolis:
seward •
longfellow •
standish •

eat

e2 > a baker's wife
     pastry shop
e6 > birchwood cafe
e12 > colossal cafe
e37 > the craftsman

shop

st. paul:
- ## snelling / hamline
- ## merriam park

eat

shop

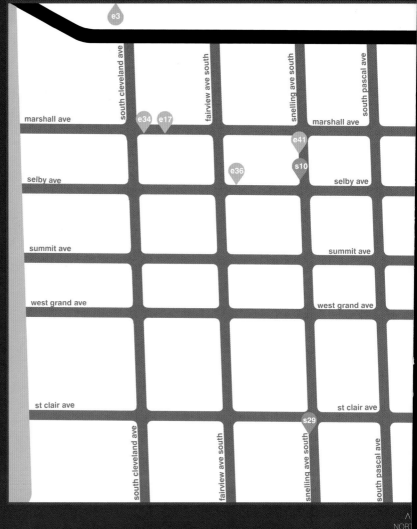

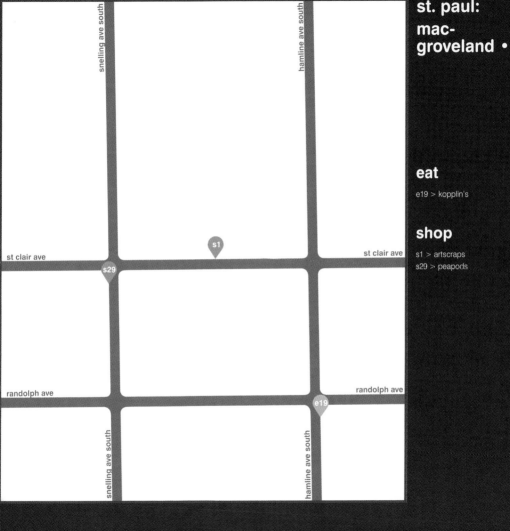

st. paul:
mac-
groveland •

eat

e19 > kopplin's

shop

s1 > artscraps
s29 > peapods

snelling ave south
hamline ave south
st clair ave
st clair ave
randolph ave
randolph ave
snelling ave south
hamline ave south

s1
s29
e19

st. paul:
• grand ave
selby / dale

eat

e14 > golden fig fine foods
e38 > the happy gnome
e39 > the lexington

shop

s3 > blackblue
s8 > cooks of crocus hill
s25 > northern brewer
s38 > the red balloon

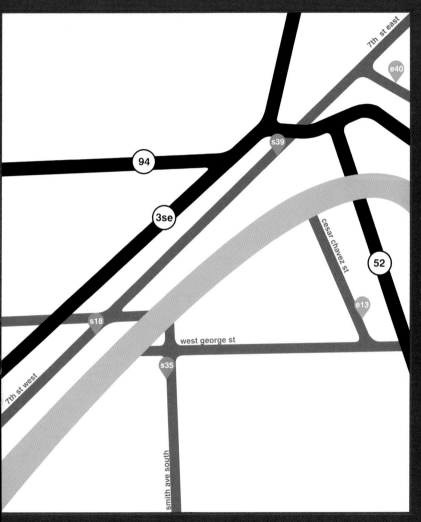

st. paul:
downtown •
west side •
dayton's
bluff •

eat

e13 > el burrito mercado
e40 > the strip club

shop

s18 > j.w. hulme co.
s35 > stormsister spatique
s39 > twin cities magic

notes

artscraps at artstart

scraps for art

1459 st. clair avenue. corner of pascal
651.698.2787 www.artstart.org
mon - fri 10a - 5p sat 10a - 4p

opened in 1988. owner: artstart
all major credit cards accepted
classes

st. paul: mac-groveland > 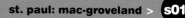 **s01**

I was trained from birth to Never Throw Anything Away because some piece of interesting paper, or unsually shaped bottle, or pretty ribbon scrap, might be useful for a future craft project. While this poses some problems for storage, organization and general cleanliness in the home, it means you always have an enormous cache of art supplies on hand. If you can't or just don't want to follow this semi-hoarding mentality, you could go to *Artscraps*, where you can find a whole plethora of those saved-from-being-tossed-crafty gems.

covet:
old knitting needles
kodak slides
bottle caps
frame corners
pine cones
yarns
bulk paper
magnetic strips

bella lana

beautiful yarn

21 fourth street se. between hennepin and central
612.331.3330 www.beautifulyarn.com
see website for hours

opened in 2007. owners: cornelia griffin and karin blomstrand
all major credit cards accepted
online shopping. classes

minneapolis: northeast > 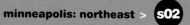 **s02**

I've become very competitive with my sisters when it comes to knitting. Each of us tries to outdo the others with our latest creations (though none will admit to the tacit contest). This probably wasn't what my mom had in mind when she taught us to knit in the first place, but we're sisters and competition is expected. I've got a competitive edge though, thanks to a nifty secret resource I have and they don't: *Bella Lana*. This shop's incredible selection of yarns and well-chosen books will help make me the top sista knitta. Check out *Bella Lana*—but don't tell my sibs, okay?

covet:
yarns:
  blue sky alpacas
  debbie bliss
  misti alpaca
  lorna's laces
  malabrigo
  twinkle
ka bamboo needles

blackblue

smart style for guys (and shoes for all)

614 selby avenue. between dale and kent

www.blkblu.com

tue - sun noon - 9p

opened in 2009. owner: steve kang

all major credit cards accepted

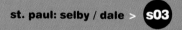

st. paul: selby / dale > s03

I was driving through St. Paul when I spied an intriguing store window on Selby Avenue. I swung my car around in the patented *eat.shop* "I need to check that place out illegal u-turn" move. There's always the niggling worry that this type of hip-jerk scouting will backfire, but *BlackBlue*, which was newly opened, had the goods. I was just as excited about the fantastic stuff for guys this place stocks as I was about discovering *BlackBlue*. Though I do not advocate illegal driving moves, I absolutely encourage you to check this coolness out.

covet:
f-troupe
penguin
superga
tretorn
woolrich
fred perry
c.c. filson co.
hyden yoo

bluebird boutique

women's clothing and accessories

3909 west 50th street. between france and halifax
952.746.8675 www.bluebirdboutique.com
mon - fri 10a - 6p sat 11a - 5p sun noon - 5p

opened in 2004. owners: allison mowery and sacha martin
all major credit cards accepted
online shopping

minneapolis: 50th and france > 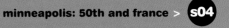 **s04**

When it comes to fashion, everybody has a belief system. I, for one, believe that the right accessories make the outfit, and this is one of the reasons I flock to *Bluebird Boutique*. The clothing here appeals to me greatly, but it's BB's accessories that ring my bell—vintage belts, drapey scarves, long hanging necklaces, fun costume jewelry and cocktail rings and good shoes (that come from sister shop *Ladyslipper*). No need to match your bag to your shoes and belt here—at *Bluebird*, it's about creating a personal style that's as free as a bird.

covet:
la made
jodi arnold
j brand
lna t's
twelfth street by cynthia vincent
vince
fluxus
bobi

brown & greene

memorable floral and gifts

4400 beard avenue south. corner of 44th
612.928.3778 www.bgfloral.net
mon - fri 10a - 6p sat 10a - 5p

opened in 1991. owner: lyn williams
all major credit cards accepted
custom orders

minneapolis: linden hills > 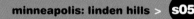 **s05**

As I stare out the window at the desolate grays and muddy colors of winter all being coated in a fresh white coat of thick falling snow and think how far away spring is, I remember that winter needn't be so glum. Just walking into *Brown & Greene* will make you feel like winter will soon be turning to spring. By the time this book hits shelves, spring flowers will be upon us, and *Brown & Greene's* offerings will be even more lush and verdant. Spring, summer, winter or fall, this little florist will always be on hand to help with seasonal malaise.

covet:
potted plants
pre de provence soaps
ribbons
candles
birdcages
potting cages
feathers

calhoun cycle

an unusual bike shop

3342 hennepin avenue south. between 33rd and 34th
612.827.8000 www.calhouncycle.com twitter: @calhouncycle
mon - fri 9a - 8p sat 9a - 7p sun 10a - 6p

opened in 1991. owner: luke breen
visa. mc
online shopping. rentals. events. repairs

minneapolis: uptown > 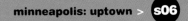 **s06**

I've been wanting a city bike for several years now, but the thing that always stops me from buying the bike is the fear of parking my beautiful new wheels on the street, leaving it chained to a post to beg some ne'er-do-well, "Steal me, steal me!" But now I don't have such a dire outlook: *Calhoun Cycle* carries an array of cool city bikes, including a folding bike, so I won't have to leave my baby chained and vulnerable and I can also take it on the bus or train. Snap! *Calhoun Cycle* is kind of taking the fun out of being a worrywart, but I'm okay with that.

covet:
bikes:
  civia
  airnimal
  brompton
  dahon
  bacchetta
  linus
  bullitt

city salvage

found and salvaged goods
507 first avenue ne. between fifth and seventh
612.627.9107 www.citysalvage.com
mon - sat 10:30a - 5:30p

opened in 1998. owner: john eckley
all major credit cards accepted

minneapolis: northeast > 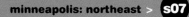 **s07**

Why does anyone bother to make anything new? Okay, I already know the answer to that question and I'm glad there are creative folks out there who make interesting, useful new things. But when I find myself at a place like *City Salvage*, I don't know why anybody would ever go to a hardware store for a cheapo plain Jane doorknob when you can get one here with character, history and patina. In fact, why buy a newfangled electronic food scale when you can get one here that's incredibly beautiful and still works after half a century. Built to last is where it's at.

covet:
architectural artifacts
vintage scale
old doorknobs
stained glass windows
street signs
dr. sign
pabst blue ribbon sign
wooden door

cooks of crocus hill

everything your kitchen ever needed

sp: 877 grand avenue. between victoria and milton
e: 3925 west 50th street. between halifax and france
651.228.1333 / 952.285.1903 www.cooksofcrocushill.com
see website for hours

opened in 1973. owners: karl benson and marie dwyer
all major credit cards accepted
online shopping. classes. registries

st paul: grand avenue / minneapolis: 50th and france > **s08**

Maybe there was a time when cooking was a humdrum, mundane task—something along the lines of mouths that had to be fed, meals that had to be made. These days, many people are throwing themselves into the art and craft of cooking and using a multitude of tools and equipment. If you are one of these folks or you just cook for the joy of it, *The Cooks of Crocus Hill* calls your name. Though my own kitchen cupboards are brimming with various utensils and devices, I always find myself coveting—or needing—something at this store. What is a painter without a brush, after all?

covet:
le creuset everything
best manufacturers pizza peel
totally bamboo cutting boards
microplane zesters
sci potato ricer
kuhn rikon cookie press
salt box
vermont slate cheese server

crafty planet

craft supplies and kits

2833 johnson street ne. between 28th and 29th
612.788.1180 www.craftyplanet.com twitter: @craftyplanet
mon - sat 10a - 7p sun 11a - 5p

opened in 2003. owners: trish hoskins and matt devries
all major credit cards accepted
online shopping. classes

minneapolis: audubon park > s09

After this stretch of wretched economy, I have noticed two trends: crafts and end-of-the-world movies. The second trend is all about destruction, the first is all about creating and being resourceful. After a run of seeing the movies about blowing each other up or destroying the climate so the world caves in on itself, I think I'll stick to crafts. Consider *Crafty Planet* instead of that Cormac McCarthy film fest of doom. Crafts are booming right now, and if need be, we might be able to stitch and glue ourselves back together with just a few supplies and instruction from here.

covet:
subversive stitchery
oliver + s patterns
fabrics
yarn
wool roving
rick rack
amy butler patterns
knitting needles

flirt

a lingerie boutique
177 north snelling avenue. corner of selby
651.698.3692 www.flirt-boutique.com
mon - sat 10a - 7p sun noon - 5p

opened in 2008. owner: jessica gerard
all major credit cards accepted

st. paul: snelling / hamline > **s10**

There are certain names that are super popular monikers for businesses. For example *Lola*, *Bliss* and *Flirt* in some form or another have all popped up on our national *eat.shop* radar. And though I have found a *Flirt* in nearly every city I visit, this *Flirt* stands out above all the others and will be the first *Flirt* to make it into an *eat.shop* book for this reason: the lingerie selections here are a blend of sexy and pragmatic, there's lots of enticing pieces here to choose from. So congratulations *Flirt*, you've broken the mold!

covet:
elle macpherson
wacoal
b.tempted
cosabella
eberjay
hanky panky
maria evora bathsalts
the laundress

grethen house netc.

stalwart women's shop

4930 france avenue south. between 49th and 50th
952.926.8725 www.grethenhouse.com twitter: @grethenhouse
mon - fri 10a - 5:30p sat 11a - 5p

opened in 1981. grethen house owner: mary brindley netc owner: nancy heidman
all major credit cards accepted

minneapolis: 50th and france >

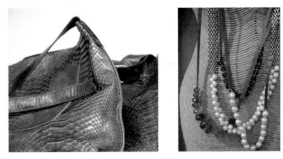

In the world of boutiques, places come and go, barely registering on the radar before they're closing up shop. Retail is a tough business, and it's one that takes always staying on top of and ahead of the game. For this reason, I am constantly in awe of *Grethen House Netc*. With their laser-sharp eye focused on every detail of clothing (*Grethen House*) and accessories (*Netc*), this team knows what their customers want, and this has made *GH* a stalwart in the Twin Cities. More than being memorable, this store is truly essential for followers of cutting-edge fashion.

covet:
yigal azrouel
chan luu
rozae by rozae nichols
rick owens
hache
zero + maria cornejo
maison martin margiela
lutz & patmos

hunt & gather

grounds for serious hunting and gathering

4944 xerxes avenue south. between 49th and 50th
612.455.0250 www.huntandgatherantiques.com
mon - sat 10:30a - 5:30p sun noon - 5p

opened in 2003. owner: kristi stratton
visa. mc

minneapolis: southwest > 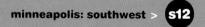 **s12**

I have always loved to hunt for things. From shark teeth on the sandy beaches of Florida and sand dollars in the salty ocean to Petosky stones on the shores of Lake Michigan. And my favorite hunting involves looking for special treasures at *Hunt & Gather*. I find it hard-as-heck to leave this place, but when I do I'm lugging a bag full of gathered finds. And here's the thing to remember at *H&G*: don't come here with a mind set on something because you'll ruin the fun of the hunt. Instead, set your mind free and explore, and you'll certainly bag many trophies.

covet:
silver napkin rings
vintage buttons
old stamps
antlers
old flash cards
silver platters
feed sacks
lots of things you didn't know you wanted

i like you

local, handcrafted goods
501 first avenue northeast. corner of fifth
612.208.0249 www.ilikeyouonline.com twitter: @ilikeyoumpls
tue - fri 11a - 7p sat 10a - 6p sun noon - 5p

opened in 2009. owners: angela lessman and sarah sweet
visa. mc
classes

minneapolis: northeast > 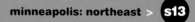 **s13**

When I sit down to write, which is what I do for a living, I'm often thinking of something else I want to be doing, like spending time in my craft room. This is when vocation and avocation live apart. But when they come together, it's a happy-making collision, which I think is the reason that Angela was so cheerful and bubbly when I met her. At *I Like You*, the ladies have pulled together a ton of cool artisan-designed pieces, many from local talents, and they also show their own work as well. It's hard to not grin and say to Angela and Sarah, "I like you too!

covet:
earwax circus
hunks of cake
duckie uglings
giraffe
hazel & melvin's room
amy rice
lovely minneapolis
emily kircher recycling artist

129

ingebretsen's

scandinavian gifts and food

1601 east lake street. corner of 16th
612.729.9333 www.ingebretsens.com
mon - fri 9a - 5:30p sat 9a - 5p

opened in 1921. owners: charles ingebretsen and warren dahl
all major credit cards accepted
online shopping

minneapolis: midtown / phillips > 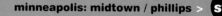 **s14**

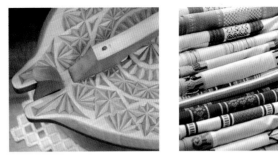

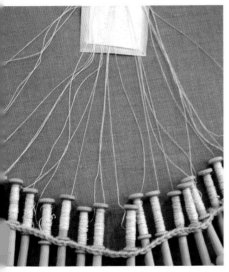

I think of the Swedes, and Scandinavians in general, as being vigorous, industrious people with a killer design sense. To see where I'm coming from, head to *Ingebretsen's*. This general store features everything from teapot cozies to Royal Copenhagen china to really good cookies and lots in betweens. And though Scandinavian design has become quite chic over the last decade—good design has been a hallmark of this region for a long time—*Ingebretsen's* covers the gamut, from the classics to the more modern items. Personally, I love it all.

covet:
embroidery kits
dala horses
nine-hold ebleskiver pan
teacake pan
lefse starter kit
outdoor meal kit
scandinavian mailbox
tokheim stoneware bowls

intoto

upscale fashion for men and women
3105 hennepin avenue south. corner of 31st
612.822.2414 www.intotogetdressed.com
mon - fri 10a - 7p sat 11a - 6p sun noon - 5p

opened in 1989. owners: mike pickart and karen heithoff
all major credit cards accepted

minneapolis: uptown > 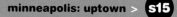 **s15**

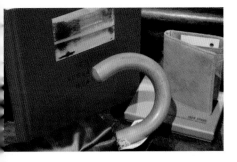

I'm crazy about London, and when I visit, which isn't often enough, I wish I could transport back with me that Brit sense of chic whether it be the tweedy, perfectly tailored gentlemanly look or the stylish, yet understated urban girl look. *Intoto*, though as far away from London geographically as one can imagine, has a brilliant array of these types of iconic looks. No wonder this place has been around for so many years. I'm clearly not the only one who realizes that *Intoto's* fashion-forward point of view is a rare and uncommon thing to find in a boutique.

covet:
etro
marni
nili lotan
dries van noten
rogues gallery
rogan
paul smith
leigh & luca

ivy

cool and funky looks for women
1440 west lake street. between holmes and hennepin
612.827.2764 www.shopivy.com twitter: @ivy_uptown
mon - sat 11a - 8p sun noon - 5p

opened in 2005. owner: ini iyamba
all major credit cards accepted

minneapolis: uptown > 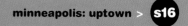 **s16**

I think there was a period of time, probably during my teenage years, when I uttered the phrase, "Everybody else is doing it," quite a few times. It didn't really work for me back then, and now when I see businesses following that same premise, I see that it's not working for them either. Ini is someone who clearly follows his own path, and it shows at his store *Ivy*. When you shop here, you'll find clothing and accessories that aren't in every other store in town. Though I'm not one to follow, I would be all ears when it came to Ini's sage advice about all things stylish.

covet:
dvf
213
jaipur
toki doki
liquid
alexis hudson
seychelles
black halo

june

stylish women's consignment store
3406 lyndale avenue south. between 34th and 35th
612.354.3970 www.juneresale.com
tue - thu noon - 6:30p fri - sat noon - 6pm

opened in 2008. owner: duane stinson
all major credit cards accepted

minneapolis: southwest > 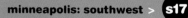 **s17**

If you associate consignment shops with stuffy places crammed so full of stuff that they make you feel anxious and confused, scratch that association before coming to *June* as it's the polar opposite. This is a perfect little boutique of a shop, set up like any store selling desirable goods should be: thoughtfully and with order, reason and inspiration. If you feel like you must have an association with *June*, associate it with the fact that your wallet won't feel as light as it might after shopping at a full-price boutique.

covet:
ysl scarf
mink stoles
stella mccartney for le sport sac bag
black chloe bag
chanel flats
fiorentini and baker boots
chanel bag
louis vuitton skirt

j.w. hulme co.

classically crafted bags, gun cases and accessories

678 west seventh street. corner of st. claire
651.222.7359 www.jwhulmeco.com
see website for hours

opened in 1905. owners: chuck bidwell and jen guarino
all major credit cards accepted
online shopping

st. paul: west side > 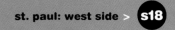 s18

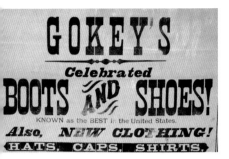

My husband announced to me recently that he wants to get his guns from his parents' home and start putting them to use by hunting for next year's Thanksgiving turkey. While I'm not quite understanding where this hunt will take place as we live in a condo in the middle of the city, I might be able to accept this plan of action if he gets a gun bag from *J.W. Hulme*. I'm in love with all of the bags from here—for travel, everyday and well, storing and carrying guns—as they truly are pieces of art. Looks like I might be into this hunting thing after all.

covet:
j.w. hulme co.:
  shoulder excursion
  magnum messenger
  overnight briefcase
  legacy handbag
  leather weekend rolling satchel
  gun cases
  classic shell bag

kilroys

reworked vintage slot machines and more
219 north second street. between second and third
612.339.5848 www.classicmalt.com
mon - fri 11a - 7p sat noon - 5p

opened in 1975. owner: kevin hammerbeck
visa. mc

minneapolis: north loop / warehouse > 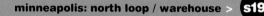 **s19**

Here's my big pronouncement for 2010: I have NOT seen it all. Until I wandered into *Kilroys*, I had begun to think that in my varied travels I had kind of covered the shopping gamut. But I've never seen anything like this huge place filled with vintage entertainment machines, including a cool British slot machine, a fortune-teller nearly identical to the one in the movie *Big* and a zillion other old-fashioned contraptions that Kevin has kept alive and in working order. It's a wonderland of mechanical gizmos that will make even the most jaded shopper smile.

covet:
slot machines
soda machines
jukeboxes
popcorn machines
neon signs
old gas pumps
vintage scale
chrome stools

ladyslipper boutique

lovely women's shoe shop
4940 france avenue south. between 49th and 50th
952.224.1900
mon - fri 10a - 6p sat 11a - 5p

opened in 2008. owner: amanda rose, sacha martin and allison mowery
all major credit cards accepted

minneapolis: 50th and france >

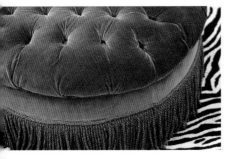

Do you believe in reincarnation? I think I might after I discovered *Ladyslipper.* When I first walked by the store, I had to do a double take: it was like seeing the ghost of one of Chicago's now-shuttered, best shoe stores—the extraordinary *Josephine.* I was immediately intrigued and couldn't help but be drawn in. Turns out, *Ladyslipper* repurposed *Josephine's* memorable interiors, carrying over a piece of its legacy while at the same time creating a fresh shopping experience focusing on affordable, yet stylish shoes. This is recycling at its finest.

covet:
shoes:
  elizabeth & james
  loeffler randall
  twelfth street by cynthia vincent
  dolce vita
  sam edelman
  frye
botkier handbags

lunalux

custom letterpress and card shop

1618 harmon place. on loring park
612.373.0526 www.lunalux.com twitter: @lunalux
tue - sat 11a - 6p

opened in 1993. owner: jenni undis
all major credit cards accepted
custom design / orders

minneapolis: loring park > **s21**

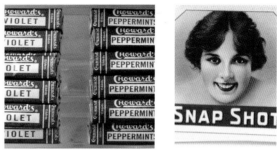

Junk mail. I'm constantly trying to eradicate it from my life. If I could only lessen the mail I don't want and increase the mail I do want. What type of mail would I want, you ask? Something that was written on a letterpress product from *Lunalux*. Nothing is more exciting to me than receiving a beautiful, letterpress card which I will pin to my bulletin board so I can gaze at it daily. Friends, don't keep me waiting, send me something from *Lunalux*. If you don't, I'm going to come here and treat myself. Actually, even if you do, I'm still stocking up here.

covet:
lunalux letterpress paper goods
notepad triad
lotta jansdotter sticky notes
letterpress posters
deluxe scratch pads
notebook cahiers
sukie sticky notes
candy!

martin patrick 3

essentials for mankind

121 north first street. between first and second
612.746.5329 www.martinpatrick3.com twitter: @martinpatrick3
mon - fri 10a - 7p sat 10a - 6p sun noon - 5p

opened in 2008. owner: greg walsh
all major credit cards accepted

minneapolis: north loop / warehouse > **s22**

I'm a sucker for gift guides. I look forward to the holidays when magazine, newspaper and online editors gather together their list of favorite things—it's like having somebody pre-shop for you. *Martin Patrick 3* feels like the living embodiment of a well-edited gift guide for men. Within ten minutes here, I could have gathered the perfect presents for my husband, father, brother and brothers-in-law. Heck, I could get so carried away here I might just buy a couple of extra things to give to the first lucky guys I walk by on the street.

covet:
vintage cuff links
baekgaard oilcloth bags
barleycorn shave set
vintage books
tokyo bay watches
faux croc pencil set
zebra wood desk accessories
pierrepont hicks ties

mitrebox

frame studio and card shop

213 washington avenue north. between second and third
612.676.0696 www.mitreboxframing.com
mon - fri 10a - 6p sat 10a - 5p

opened in 1998. owners: mary fajack and sara nachreiner
all major credit cards accepted
custom orders

minneapolis: north loop / warehouse >

Why is framing something I have such a hard time doing? I see a piece of art, love it, buy it, imagine where I'm going to hang it and even how I'll frame it. And then the piece sits. And sits. And sits longer. Unframed, unloved, unhung. It's one of those to-do list items that seems to always end up last. No more! *Mitrebox* makes me long to frame. Coming here is the furthest thing from a task or a chore; instead it's a whopping treat! Plus, there are so many other fun things here like beautiful cards and unique gifties. If only someone could make a trip to the dry cleaners a bit more enticing.

covet:
frames!
bari zaki cards
luxo banho soap
printed matter notecards
carrot & stick press cards
pancake & frank cards
weekly cupcakes

nola home

new and old global finds

404 penn avenue south. off of route 394
612.374.4066
tue - fri 10a - 6p sat 10a - 5p

opened in 2006. owner: kelly dorsey
all major credit cards accepted

minneapolis: bryn mawr > 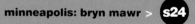 **s24**

Although I love to go along with my husband on his international trips, one of my favorite things about him going solo is when he comes home, and I get to dig through his suitcase and discover the various treasures he has found on his travels. It's a blast to see what he sniffed out and thought was worthy to bring back. When I visit *Nola Home,* it feels like I'm back in my husband's suitcase, except it's a really big suitcase and there's a ton more to discover. Kelly has a great eye and when she goes a-travelin', I know I'll want what she has found.

covet:
aviary prints
carving sets
salad serving sets
buddhas
beads
wooden stools
wicker chair
rugs

northern brewer

homebrew supply

1150 grand avenue. between dunlap and lexington
651.789.0189 www.northernbrewer.com twitter: @northern_brewer
mon - fri 10a - 7p sat 10a - 5p sun noon - 3p

opened in 1999. owner: chris farley
visa. mc
online shopping

st paul: grand avenue >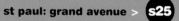

It's been a rough couple of years for a lot of people, and DIY—which started out as a hobby for hipsters—is now an essential fact of life for many people. I don't want to sound all doom and gloom because this do-it-yourself thing can be pretty darn fun. For example, brewing your own beer is a hoot (what other hobby includes a fermenator?). Worried that it's too much work? It's really not, especially when there's *Northern Brewer* waiting with all the right supplies. Whether you're feeling sappy, happy or just plain hoppy, *Northern Brewer* is the spot to get your brewing gear.

covet:
barley crusher
14 gallon fermenator
blichmann autosparge
grain malts
hops
starter kits
kegging equipment
bottles & caps

oscar & belle

organic baby clothing

2812 west 43rd street. between upton and vincent
612.216.3738 www.oscarandbelle.com twitter: @oscarandbelle
mon - sat 10a - 6p sun noon - 4p

opened in 2009. owner: anna gustafson
all major credit cards accepted
online shopping

minneapolis: linden hills > 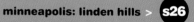

As my husband and I prepare for our first baby, we have in place a general approach when it comes to buying stuff for the little bambino: neutral colors and as organic as possible. To some, this might sound pretty fussbudgety, but isn't this preferable to having your fresh new baby swathed in synthetic materials or sucking on unnatural substances? Yessss, it is. At *Oscar & Belle*, the organic baby goods are a-plenty, and most are in soothing hues. So whether we have an Oscar or a Belle (not telling), I can guarantee you there will be some *O&S* in his/her life.

covet:
oscar & belle:
  organic skincare
  baby carriers
  custom bedding & pillows
  clothing from newborn to size 6
natural rubber pacifier
imps & elfs striped socks
egg certified organic clothing

pacifier

gifts and goods for baby

310 east hennepin avenue. between university and fourth
612.623.8123 www.pacifieronline.com
see website for hours and second location

opened in 2004. owners: wing tran and jon witthuhn
all major credit cards accepted
online shopping. registries

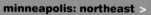 **minneapolis: northeast >** s27

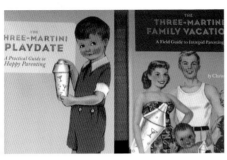

There are a lot of things about being pregnant that aren't fun: morning sickness, an ever-expanding waistline and an ever-shrinking view of my toes. But there are pluses, like *Pacifier*—a place that makes me focus on the cool gear I am going to get for the kiddo instead of the aches and pains and girth involved with growing the kiddo. So if you're feeling the nine-month woes and questioning whether your baby will ever want to come out of your comfy womb, come to *Pacifier*, do some shopping and grab yourself a sweet, quease-squelching preggie pop as you browse.

covet:
wee-go glass bottles
boon snack ball
beaba babycook
beaba multi portions tray
offi nest bassinet
halo sleepsack
dwell studio sleepsacks
tooli candela set

parc boutique

women's stylish basics

328 east hennepin avenue. between university and fourth
612.353.4966 www.parcboutique.com twitter: @parcboutique
see website for hours

opened in 2008. owner: thao bui
visa. mc

minneapolis: northeast > 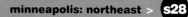s28

When I walked in here the first time, my attention was caught immediately by the gorgeous robin's egg blue and cream Vespa. All I could think about was the girl that would ride this Vespa around town. In my mind, she would wear clothing that wasn't screamingly trendy, but still unmistakenly stylish. Obviously this girl would shop at *Parc*, where you can find everyday essentials that ad spunk to a wardrobe. I'm just wondering if I buy enough here, would Thao consider giving a gift with purchase? I was thinking the Vespa would be nice...

covet:
alternative apparel
splendid
la made
gypsy 05
velvet
fluxus
trinity
nation

peapods

natural toys and baby care
251 snelling avenue south. between st. clair and berkeley
651.695.5559 www.peapods.com twitter: @peapodsnatural
mon - sat 10a - 6p

opened in 1999. owner: millie adelsheim and dan marshall
all major credit cards accepted
online shopping

st. paul: mac-groveland >

The cloth diaper world has become ridiculously complicated. Back in ye olde days you had to deal with just a flat piece of cloth and big metal diaper pins. Today, if you want to use cloth to cover your baby's tush you must choose: prefolds or flat, all-in-ones or pockets, liners, covers, pins or clips, velcros or snaps. I'm so confused. *Peapods* to the rescue. There's a diaper wall here that clarifies and simplifies the choices. Phew. And once you've dealt with choosing a stinky stuff containment system, you'll have loads of time to explore the other great things at this eco-friendly spot.

covet:
kicky pants
aden + anais swaddles
haba toys
burt's bees baby bee
beka maple blocks
green toys recycled sand toys
fair trade knit hacky sacks
remo lollipop drum

rewind

a look back at fashion

2829 johnston street northeast. between 28th and 29th
612.788.9870 www.rewindminneapolis.com
mon - sat 11a - 7p sun 11a - 5p

opened in 2006. owner: sarah hoese
visa. mc

minneapolis: audubon park > 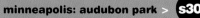 **s30**

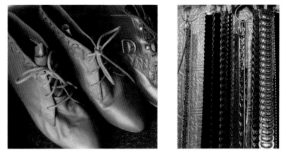

Ahhh, to be able to rewind. Like when you got that mess of a perm in the early '90s or wore a purple satin prom dress, or said that nasty thing to your mom when you were nine. If we could, we would << like a cassette player, but unfortunately humans are stuck on >>. We can, though, rewind when it comes to fashion and wear clothing from the past in a modern way. Hence, the reason you'll want to visit *Rewind*. Here you'll find some of the greatest hits of the past that deserve a new life in the future. So get over that purple satin faux pas, and move on with *Rewind*.

covet:
bangles
sunglasses
buttons
sequined tops
orange patent doc martens
gold belts
color-coded everything
brown leather & wool ankle boots

roam

modern goods for your home

813 glenwood avenue. between bryant and lyndale
612.377.6465 www.roaminteriors.com
mon - fri 10a - 6p sat 10a - 5p

opened in 2007. owner: john stedman
all major credit cards accepted

minneapolis: north loop / warehouse > **s31**

Roam. It reminds me of words like "wander" and "stroll" and is distantly related to "relax" and "enjoy." Lately, these are words that have fallen out of my vocab and have been replaced with: Race! Hurry! Run! Speed up! Upon entering this store, I felt all those action words dissolve away, and I immediately had the desire to melt into one of the big couches or sit down and kick my shoes off at one of the dining tables. Nothing at *Roam* screamed at me to hurry up and get going. What a relief. But, if you haven't come to *Roam* yet, I'd hurry up and get here! Chop chop.

covet:
modern twist
blomus
blu dot
alessi
menu
park haus
sagaform
norman copenhagen

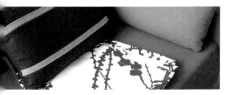

russell+hazel

things to get organized
4388 france avenue south. corner of 44th
952.279.1360 www.russellandhazel.com
mon - sat 10a - 6p sun noon - 4p

opened in 2006. owner: chris plantan
all major credit cards accepted
online shopping

minneapolis: 50th and france >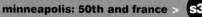

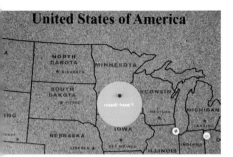

Buying back-to-school supplies was one of my favorite activities growing up, second only to Christmas morning. I loved perusing the store with my list of needed tools, checking off each as I went: One box No. 2 pencils—check. Five trapper keepers—check. One pink pearl eraser—check. If only I would have been able to shop at *Russell+Hazel*, my school supplies dreams would have all come true. But wait, it's not too late, because *R+H* has all the things I lust after as an adult—products that make organization fun and look good at the same time. It's better than Christmas morning here.

covet:
russell+hazel:
  binders & files
  composition book
  sticky notes
  leather pencil case
  mini pattern binders
  smartdate system
  recipe card keeper

salon rouge

beauty shop and salon
6 south 13th street. between hennepin and harmon
612.374.2201 www.salonrougempls.com
tue - thu 9a - 8p fri 9a - 6p sat 9a - 3p

opened in 2005. owners: richard staab
all major credit cards accepted

minneapolis: downtown >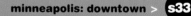

I am a wreck. Angry hangnails on every finger, nails uneven and peeling, feet rough enough to sand with, split ends multiplying like bunnies, eyebrows like Andy Rooney's. Either Calgon needs to take me away or I need all of the beauty products from *Salon Rouge* to help me in my desperate time of need. Richard sources the best beauty products from around the world, each of them designed to make you look and feel like a beautiful creature. And if the pretty products don't do the trick, then you'll need to partake in the salon services here. I plan to.

covet:
kevyn aucoin makeup
apple & bee
phyto
bumble and bumble
antica farmacista
pre de provence
comme des garçons
roger & gallet

shoppe local*

locally sourced gifts and goods
813 west 50th street. between aldrich and bryant
612.827.3071 www.patinastores.com
mon - sat 9:30a – 9p sun 11a - 6p

opened in 2009. owners: christine ward and rick haase
all major credit cards accepted
*please check website to see if shoppe local has re-opened

minneapolis: tangletown > 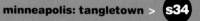 **s34**

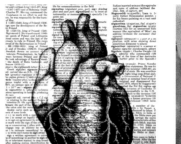

For seven years now the *eat.shop* guides have been proclaiming this simple statement: We love local. And why is this? Because without local businesses, all cities would be one big maze of corporate outposts. Can you imagine what it would be like to have the eating and shopping choices in your town be exactly the same as what you would find in thousands of other cities around the world? Thank goodness there's a big surge behind supporting locally owned businesses like *Shoppe Local*, which is doubly special because the goods it sells are all made locally. We love *Shoppe Local*!

covet:
minnetonka moccasins
ames farm honey
j. r. watkins lip balm
block bots
jane jenni plates
crafterall topo for the wall

stormsister spatique

naturally luxe beauty products
635 south smith avenue. between king and baker
612.716.5480 www.stormsister.biz twitter: @stormsister
mon - fri 10a - 5p sat - sun 10a - 2p

opened in 2006. owner: becky sturm
all major credit cards accepted
online shopping

st. paul: west side >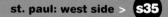

Organic is everywhere these days. Organic food, organic diapers, organic toothpaste, organic motor-cycle brake pads (?!). Though some businesses use organic as a marketing tool, other businesses walk the talk, like this little shop. *Stormsister Boutique* has sourced some of the most interesting eco-healthy beauty products available. So even if you find it hard to make the switch to organic, this place will help going green incredibly easy. At the same time, it will help you feel healthier about yourself and the products you use.

covet:
dresdner essenz sparkling bath
intelligent nutrients everything
ted gibson hair sheet
fleur's aroma minéral poudre d'or
phytocéane bain d'eau
john masters organics shampoo
principessa bellissima bar
babybearshop organic lip balm

style minneapolis

beautiful home shop

4501 nicollet avenue south. corner of 45th
612.377.3331
wed - sat noon - 6p

opened in 2003. owner: shayne barsness
all major credit cards accepted

minneapolis: kingfield >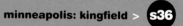

There are certain things that seem easy but actually require skill to do well. For example, it seems easy to put lights on the xmas tree i.e., throwing the whole wad of lights on the tree willy nilly. In reality, it's an art to get the strands evenly spaced and wrapped around the tree in a harmonic way. Shayne understands this fine art of balance, and it shows at *Style Minneapolis*. From her own line of jewelry to the found objects and vintage pieces she repurposes in a glorious way, Shane has that magic ability to make everything seem special.

covet:
shayne & coco jewelry
vintage dominoes
french thread
linen pillows
feathers
antique silver platters
silverplate knives, spoons, forks
shayne's style!

175

tangletown gardens

garden store and urban oasis

5353 nicollet avenue. corner of 54th
612.822.4769 www.tangletowngardens.com
check website for hours

opened in 2002. owner: scott endres and dean engelmann
all major credit cards accepted
landscape design. csa shares. delivery. custom potting

minneapolis: tangletown > **s37**

It's hard to face the facts: I have a brown thumb. There, I've said it. I've been in denial for years because my parents are both talented gardeners and have grown and sustained a gorgeous, lush garden—hence why I've always been convinced that someday my green thumb gene would emerge. Alas, it hasn't. I'm likely to kill most anything green despite my dreams of creating a Secret-Garden-like environment. I'm not going to give up, though, and *Tangletown Gardens* is my inspiration. With their supplies, gear and books, I may be able to train my sorry excuse for a thumb.

covet:
jumbo starter clematis
small succulents
anything potted!
gardening books
farm fresh goods:
  happy chicken eggs
  ruby queen red corn
  tangled beans

the red balloon bookshop

fantastic children's book shop

891 grand avenue. between milton and victoria
651.224.8320 www.redballoonbookshop.com
mon - fri 10a - 8p sat 10a - 6p sun noon - 5p

opened in 1984. owners: carol erdahl and michele cromer-poiré
visa. mc
online shopping. storytimes

st paul: grand avenue > s38

I have recently been to a plethora of book-themed baby showers. Every time I get one of these invitations I'm torn. Part of me feels that I want to buy the classics like *Winnie The Pooh* and *Blueberries for Sal*. But then I love love love the new classics like *Charley Harper's ABCs*. There's really no need for me to angst as *The Red Balloon* carries both within its thoughtful collection. Amongst the stacks here you'll find teenagers, toddlers, adults and all ages in-between because there's something for everyone. And the one thing they all have in common is a big love of books.

covet:
happy baby 123 by roger priddy
my one hundred adventures by polly horvath
beatrix potter books
the humblebee hunter by deborah hopkinson
the runaway bunny by margaret wise brown
hot rod hamster by derek anderson
schoolhouse rock dvd
going bovine by libba bray

twin cities magic & costume co.

crazy costume shop

250 seventh street east. between wall and wacouta
651.227.7888 www.twincitiesmagic.com
mon - fri 10a - 6p sat 10a - 5p

opened in 1986. owners: jim berg and fred baisch
all major credit cards accepted

st paul: downtown >

My brother and his wife named their son Johnny Utah after the Keanu Reeves character in the movie *Point Break*. They've mentioned that a second son might be dubbed Bodie after—yes, you guessed it—the surfer dude played by Patrick Swayze who robs banks with a crew wearing masks of the U.S. Presidents. I'm thinking a future gift for this family should be some Reagan, Nixon and Clinton masks from *Twin Cities Magic & Costume*. This place is an unbelievable resource for costumes of any kind, whether your disguise needs be devious or droll.

covet:
zillions of masks & hats
wigs
costumes
jester shoes
striped leg warmers
vulcan fire
le maitre haze machine
ben nye make-up

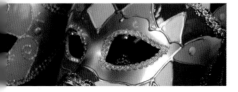

181

victory

antiques and enchanting home goods

3505 west 44th street. between beard and chowen
612.926.8200 www.shopvictory.com
tue - sat 11a - 5p

opened in 2003. owner: kerry ciardelli-olson
visa. mc

minneapolis: linden hills > **s40**

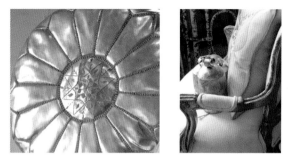

As I continue to watch my favorite stores across the country shutter their bricks-and-mortar storefronts and set up shop online, I wonder, is this the beginning of the new retail frontier? And then I come to *Victory* and realize that just as print will never be gone, extraordinary real-life stores like *Victory* will continue. The experience of being in a place like *Victory* isn't something that can be replicated virtually, walking amongst Kerry's extraordinary finds. You might, however, want to check out her blog. Though it's virtual, it will give you a look into Kerry's reality.

covet:
antique silver brush
cashmere covered hot water bottles
assorted vintage english dinner knives
venetian hand-painted zipper case
beautiful art books
english silver plate sugar tongs
victory's shea butter face & body cream
pillows & bedding

vivid home

interior designer's home shop
226 cedar lake road south. corner of oliver
612.874.3283 www.vividinteriordesign.com
mon - fri 9a - 5p sat 10a - 4p

opened in 2009. owner: danielle loven
visa. mc

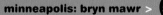

minneapolis: bryn mawr > **s41**

I have a side gig. I am a professional de-clutterer. My qualifications? I love to straighten, fold, align and dispose of. Something I've found as a clearer-outer is that usually one needs a motivation, which can come from seeing something or someplace that inspires change. *Vivid Home* is the perfect motivator. If coming into this beautiful place isn't enough to get your fires burning, then bait yourself with something even better. Upon getting rid of junk you don't need, reward yourself with a special treat from here. Is your motivation more vivid now?

covet:
k. hall designs candles & lotion
large pieces of birch bark
shell balls
hourglass
boxwood balls
glass milk jar
tall optic decanter

wonderment

wooden toys and cool crafts for kids
m: 4306 upton avenue south. between 43rd and 44th
sp: 949 grand avenue. between chatsworth and milton
www.wondermentshop.com
see website for hours

opened in 2005. owners: zuzanne fenner, lisa macmartin and joyce olson-kapell
all major credit cards accepted
online shopping. classes

minneapolis: linden hills / st. paul: grand avenue > **s42**

It's a little scary to contemplate, but there is an ever-growing subculture of little zombies that dot our landscape. Look around; you can see them everywhere. Last night at the restaurant I saw one glued to a portable dvd player at the next table. At a party last weekend, there were three zombies with glazed-over eyes, on their fifth hour of playing Nintendo. I'm pretty sure all of these kids would come back to life if they played with the toys from *Wonderment*. These are toys that get kids to use their imagination, toys that encourage their creativity to burst forth. Stop the zombification at *Wonderment*.

covet:
plan b eco doll house
jaw harp
mossy creek woodworks rattle
bunther keil animal sets
wooden vegetables & fruit
mini mesh market bag
fagus wood trucks
camden rose knitting tower

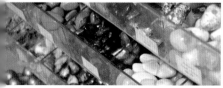

notes

etc.

the eat.shop guides were created by kaie wellman and are published by cabazon books

eat.shop twin cities 2nd edition was written, researched and photographed by anna h. blessing

editing: kaie wellman   copy editing: lynn king   fact checking: michaela cotter santen
map and layout production: julia dickey and bryan wolf.

anna thx: all of the business owners in this book. peter and emily for so warmly opening up their home. shawn for always holding up his end of the imbibing and devouring.

cabazon books: eat.shop twin cities 2nd edition
ISBN-13 9780982325452

every effort has been made to ensure the accuracy of the information in this book. however, certain details are subject to change. please remember when using the guides that hours alter seasonally and sometimes sadly, businesses close. the publisher cannot accept responsibility for any consequences arising from the use of this book.

the eat.shop guides are distributed by independent publishers group: www.ipgbook.com

to peer further into the world of eat.shop and to buy books, please visit: www.eatshopguides.com

PRINTED IN CHINA